Staying Alive

Written by Jenny Feely

sundance™

Many animals are food
for other animals.

They have many ways to keep
from being eaten by predators.

Animals That Use Speed

Kangaroos can move quickly.
They use their strong tails
to push as they jump.

Deer are very fast runners.
They try to stay away from predators
by running fast.
They jump in the air as they run.
This makes them hard to catch.

Animals That Stay in Groups

Zebras live in groups to keep safe.
The safest place is usually in the
middle of the group.
The zebras' stripes make it hard
to see one single zebra in a group.

Fish swim in big groups.
It is hard for a predator to catch
one single fish.

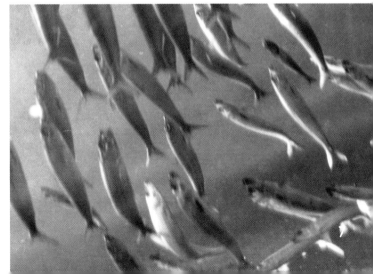

Animals That Use Armor

Echidnas are covered with sharp spines.
This makes them difficult to kill
and difficult to eat.

Turtles have a hard shell. They can hide their legs and head in their shell.

This makes them difficult to kill and difficult to eat.

Animals That Use Bluff

Toads often puff themselves up and hiss at predators. This makes them look big and fierce.

Frilled lizards hold up their frill and stand on their back legs.

This makes them seem bigger and fiercer than they are.

Animals That Use Poison

Ladybugs are bright red or yellow.
Animals with bright red or yellow
coloring don't taste good.
Predators leave them alone.

Some caterpillars are brightly colored.
They are poisonous.
Predators do not eat them.

Animals That Use Lookouts

Some monkeys watch for predators.
They make a noise when they see
a predator. All the monkeys run away.

Rabbits watch for predators.
The rabbit that is watching hits
the ground to make a noise. This warns
the other rabbits that a predator is near.

Animals That Blend In

Some seals are white.
They blend in with the snow.
This makes it hard for predators
to find and eat them.

Animals that may be eaten
by predators find many different
ways to stay alive.